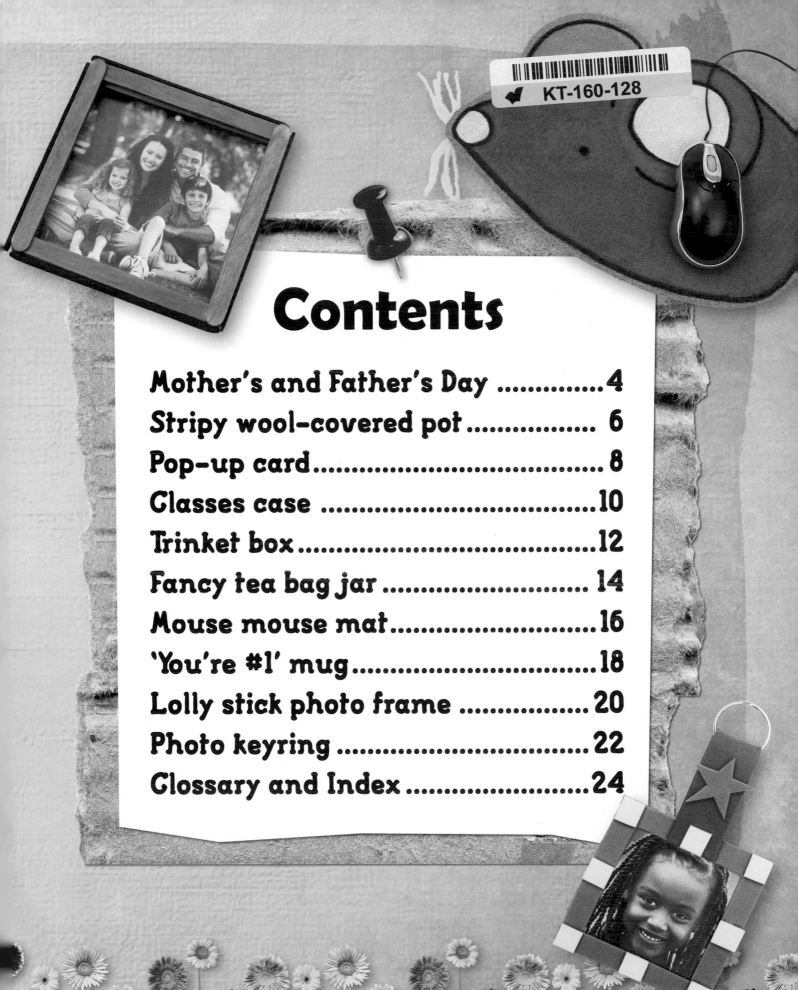

Contents

Mother's and Father's Day 4

Stripy wool-covered pot 6

Pop-up card.................................. 8

Glasses case 10

Trinket box...................................12

Fancy tea bag jar 14

Mouse mouse mat..........................16

'You're #1' mug..............................18

Lolly stick photo frame 20

Photo keyring 22

Glossary and Index 24

KT-160-128

Mother's and Father's Day

Mother's and Father's Days are a chance to show your parents how much you care. Make this year's Mother's and Father's Day gifts really unique, so they will be remembered for years to come. In this book there are lots of fun craft ideas for you to create, and lots of tips too, so you can make the most of your projects.

Trinket box: pages 12-13

We all have different hobbies and interests. Think about the person you are making the present for. Do they like certain colours or patterns? Do they love sport, or prefer going shopping? Each project in this book can be changed slightly to suit the person you are making it for. If you fancy making the lolly stick photo frame on pages 20–21, you could use colours that match their kitchen, so it fits in well when displayed on the fridge. Or if you want to make the glasses case on pages 10–11, you may decide to use your pet cat as inspiration instead.

Crafting can be messy, especially if you are using glitter or glues, so make sure you cover all your work surfaces with old newspaper or a plastic tablecloth before you begin. Always wash your hands after you have used glue to stop your works of art being ruined by sticky fingers, and ask an adult to help you with scissors or sharp compasses.

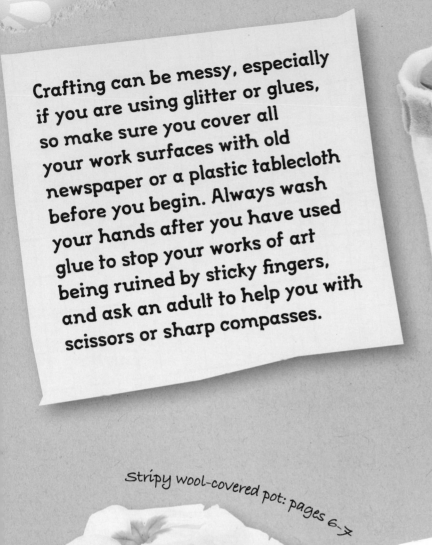

Fancy tea bag jar: Pages 14-15

Stripy wool-covered pot: pages 6-7

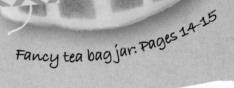

Help make Mother's Day and Father's Day extra special by creating something handmade, and have loads of fun while doing it!

Stripy wool-covered pot

These pots are brilliant for putting all sorts of things in. Make a range of them to store pens, craft materials, gadgets, or even a plant.

You will need:
- A plastic or clay pot
- PVA glue
- A paint brush
- Different-coloured wool
- Scissors

1

Turn your pot upside down and paint a thin layer of PVA glue all around the sides.

2

Wind the wool around the base of the pot (which is now at the top) until you have a stripe 1cm wide, and then cut the wool.

3

Choose another colour of wool and begin winding it around the pot, starting where the last colour ended.

4

Continue swapping colours every 1cm so that you make lots of stripes all the way up the side of the pot.

5

Cover the whole pot in another layer of PVA glue. This will dry clear and act as a varnish.

These pots can be used outside too, but make sure you coat them in three layers of outdoor varnish first, so that they are fully waterproof.

Pop-up card

This pop-up card is the perfect way to say 'thank you' to your mum or dad. It looks best when it is opened up, so remember to display it for everyone to see.

You will need:

- Coloured A4 card
- A ruler
- Scissors
- Star and dot stickers
- A silver pen
- Ribbon
- Sticky tape

1

Fold a piece of card in half and make two cuts that are 5cm long and 10cm apart from each other with your scissors.

Watch this step-by-step video of the pop-up card being made!

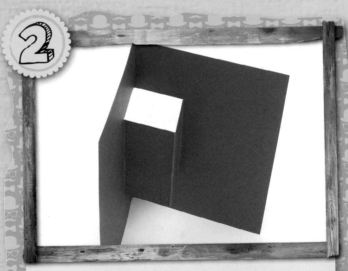

2

Open up the card and press the cut piece into the middle to make a box. This will be the pop-up present part of your card.

3

Stick lots of coloured dots onto the present part and lots of stars onto the background.

4

Draw around the present and stars using the silver pen.

5

Cut a 20cm length of ribbon and tie it into a bow. Use the sticky tape to attach the bow to the top of the present.

Put the card in an envelope, and fill it with some glitter or confetti to make it even more special when your mum or dad opens it. It will be a great surprise, and add some extra sparkle too!

9

Glasses case

This is a great gift for anyone who owns glasses or sunglasses. The adorable dog design is perfect for your mum or dad – they will be wanting one each!

You will need:

- Blue, brown, black and red felt
- A ruler
- Scissors
- Fabric glue
- A black marker pen
- Googly eyes

1

Cut a piece of blue felt into a 20cm x 20cm square, and round off the top corners.

2

Fold this in half and glue two sides together, leaving the top of the case open.

3

Cut one large circle, one medium-sized circle, two small circles, two ear shapes and a tail shape out of the brown felt.

4

Stick these onto the case in a dog shape, using the fabric glue.

5

Stick on the googly eyes then cut out a black nose and some fancy red glasses. Stick these on and leave the whole thing to dry overnight.

You can make up different designs yourself by choosing your favourite animal and making some glasses for it to wear. See how great it looks when you dress a giraffe or even a hippo in some spectacles!

Trinket box

No one will be able to guess that this beautiful boat is also a handy trinket box. You could put a token or small treat inside before you give it as a gift to someone special.

Watch this step-by-step video of the trinket box being made!

You will need:

- A small cardboard box with a lid
- Coloured card
- Scissors
- A glue stick
- Blue paper
- Blue card
- A pencil
- Grey paper
- Stripy or patterned paper

1

Cover the base and lid of the box with card. The card around the box lid should be slightly wider than the rim.

2

Cut out some wave shapes from the blue paper and stick them all around the bottom of the box.

3

Cut out a circle of blue card, sit the box on it and glue in place.

4

Use a pencil to roll a piece of grey paper into a thin tube and glue it onto the box to make a mast.

5

Cut two triangular sails out of the patterned paper and glue them onto the mast.

Disguise your trinket box as a delicious-looking cake with a pom-pom cherry on top, or even a green monster with big googly eyes and sharp teeth coming out of the lid.

Fancy tea bag jar

At first glance you might mistake this tea bag jam jar for a hot cup of tea! Use it to hold lots of different flavours of tea, and to keep the tea fresh.

You will need:

- A jam jar
- A fabric tape measure
- Green, white and yellow felt
- Scissors
- Fabric glue

Measure around your jam jar. Cut out a piece of felt that is 2cm longer than this measurement, and high enough to cover the glass part and the lid.

Glue the felt onto the jam jar.

3

Cut out another piece of felt in the same colour that is 15cm high and 2cm wide.

4

Glue this strip onto the jam jar so that it looks like a handle.

5

Cut out felt shapes to decorate your mug, and glue them in place using fabric glue.

If you have a tea bag with the string and label attached, leave it dangling out of the jam jar so that it looks like a real cup of tea.

Mouse mouse mat

This funky mouse mouse mat is the perfect gift for any computer lover.

1

Draw a mouse shape onto the cork tile using the marker pen. Make sure that the shape is large enough to fit a computer mouse on.

2

Use the scissors to cut just outside the black line, so that you have a small border around the mat.

3

Use undiluted acrylic paint to colour in the mat.

4

Cut a length of wool that is no more than 20cm long and five shorter lengths of wool that are about 10cm long.

5

Stick the long piece of wool to the back of the mat with the electrical tape to make the tail and the shorter pieces to the 'nose' to make the whiskers.

If you have a spare piece of cork, you could make a mouse mat that looks like a slice of cheese, too!

'You're #1' mug

Your mum or dad will know they're number one with this great mug that lets them know just how amazing you think they are.

You will need:
- A plain, white mug
- Ceramic paints
- Electrical tape
- A Sponge
- A black ceramic marker

1

Stick lines of electrical tape onto the mug to make the #1 shape.

2

Use the sponge to dab ceramic paint all over the mug in a thin layer.

3

Leave the paint to dry, and then carefully peel off the tape.

4

Use the ceramic marker to draw around the outline of the '#1'.

5

Some ceramic paints need to be baked in the oven to be fixed. Check the labels and follow any instructions.

Use star or dot stickers from the project on pages 8-9 instead of the tape. Stick them all over the mug, sponge over the top with a thin layer of paint and remove them before you bake the mug in the oven.

Lolly stick photo frame

Make a frame for your favourite picture and give it as a present that can be handily displayed on a fridge or any other magnetic surface.

You will need:

- Coloured lolly sticks
- Craft glue
- A photo
- Scissors
- Sticky pads
- A flat magnet

1

Glue four lolly sticks into a frame shape using the craft glue.

2

Build up two more layers of sticks on top of the frame, so that it is about 1cm deep.

3

Glue four more lolly sticks of the same colour around the edges of the frame.

4

Attach the photo to the back of the frame using the sticky pads or craft glue. You may have to trim your photo to size.

5

Finally attach the magnet to the back of the frame using the craft glue.

You can make lots of different-shaped frames. Try making a triangle or a hexagon to go with your square.

Photo keyring

Create this colourful photo frame to display your favourite photo. It can be attached to lots of different things using the handy loop.

You will need:

- Yellow, red and purple craft foam
- A black marker pen
- A ruler
- Scissors
- A photo
- Craft glue
- A split ring keyring
- Masking tape

1

Cut two 7cm x 7cm squares out of purple craft foam. Cut the middle out of one square to make a frame with a 1cm border.

2

Cut your picture down to size, and glue it onto the purple square.

3

Cut a strip of red craft foam 11cm x 2cm and thread a split ring keyring onto it. Fold the foam in half to make a loop with the ring at the top. Glue the frame to the picture, then glue the loop to the frame. Use masking tape to hold it in place while the glue dries.

4

Cut small, yellow squares and a purple star from craft foam.

You can cut the frame into different shapes. Try making a circle, a triangle or a star, too.

5

Decorate your keyring with the foam shapes, sticking them down with craft glue.

Glossary

confetti tiny pieces of coloured paper

gadget a small and useful device, such as a mobile phone

hexagon a shape with six sides

hobby an activity that people do for fun in their spare time

mast a wooden pole that supports the sails of a ship

spectacles glasses

trinket a small ornament or piece of jewellery

undiluted when something has not had water added to it

varnish a liquid that is painted onto a surface, such as wood, and dries hard and shiny, making the surface waterproof

Index

boat 12–13

cake 13
card 8–9
cat 4
computer 16
confetti 7

glasses case 4, 10–11

keyring 22–23

monster 13
mouse mat 16–17
mug 18–19

photo frame 4, 20–21, 22–23
plant pot 6–7

tea bag jar 14–15
trinket box 12–13

wool 6–7, 16, 17

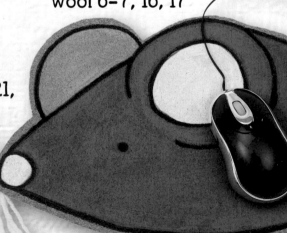

24

MOTHER'S AND FATHER'S DAY CRAFTS

ANNALEES LIM

First published in paperback in 2017 by Wayland
Copyright © Hodder and Stoughton Limited 2017

Wayland
An imprint of
Hachette Children's Group
Part of Hodder & Stoughton
Carmelite House
50 Victoria Embankment
London EC4Y 0DZ

MIX
Paper from
responsible sources
FSC® C104740

Editor: Elizabeth Brent
Craft stylist: Annalees Lim
Designer: Dynamo Ltd
Photographer: Simon Pask, N1 Studios

The website addresses (URLs) and QR codes included in this book were valid at the time
of going to press. However, it is possible that contents or addresses may have changed
since the publication of this book. No responsibility for any such changes can be accepted
by either the author or the Publisher.

ISBN   978 0 7502 8996 2
Library eBook ISBN   978 0 7502 8805 7

Printed in China

10 9 8 7 6 5 4 3 2 1

Wayland is a division of Hachette Children's Group,
an Hachette UK company.

www.hachette.co.uk

Picture acknowledgements:
All step-by-step craft photography: Simon Pask, N1 Studios;
images used throughout for creative graphics: Shutterstock